30 PROMPTS 30 STORIES BOOK 5

Let The Journey Begin

Marier Farley

Marier Farley

This book was published thanks to free support and training from:
EbookPublishingSchool.com

Acknowledgement

I would like to thank F. H. Blocker, S. N. Patterson, D. J. Patterson II, V. Z. H. Hughes, K. J. and N. J. Hughes, V. P. Hughes, Y. R. Hughes, R. E. Hughes, S. A. Hughes, and D. Patterson for helping me get finished with this book. Without your encouragement I would've stopped writing. Thank you. Special thanks go to my special sister who went on my first date with me at the age of 3 as my chaperone, M. M. D. Hughes. She will always hold a special place in my heart. She died at the age of 4.

Dedication

This book is dedicated to the ladies in green, Lula B Edwards, a beloved aunt and Brenda Joyce Logan Turner Hughes a beloved sister-in-law. Both of these ladies lost the battle with illness the first to a stroke and the second to bone cancer, but they won the war because they are home with our Lord and Savior Jesus the Christ. I will see you again.

WHY I WROTE THIS BOOK

I wrote this book because I have felt so often that a need for prompts with more detail would help many writers to create novels and or short stories that they would not have done before reading this book. I believe that by providing more than just something to spur the imagination but help direct the thought processes of people who read the prompts toward greater success.

1. While walking through the park, you locate an empty bench and sit down to people watch. After about ten minutes a woman comes along, smiles and takes a seat even though several other benches are empty. She sits beside you for fifteen minutes with her hands in her lap held tightly together. She does not speak. She then turns to you and asks you this question: "Have you ever loved someone so hard and so long yet they don't know what you are all about?" You look at her with mild interest until you realize that she wants an answer. You decide to give her a flippant answer but she holds your feet to the fire, and soon the two of you have spent two hours together. She looks at her watch and stands and says: "See you tomorrow about the same time." She walks away without waiting for your response. What do you do next? Include a backstory for both characters. Take the story to a logical conclusion. This story should be an action adventure story. Include at least two HEAs, lots of humor, and several plot twists. There should be not strong language or explicit descriptions of sex. Make this a 50,000-word story. Ensure that you explain what the two people are experiencing during this encounter.

2. A group of you return for a funeral. The deceased is one of your best bud's group. The ten of you formed a friendship during middle school and named your group The Best Buds Group. The man who died is one of the longest serving members and he died during the war and left a widow and two small children. Build your world around a small town in the south. Include interesting secondary characters who play a vital role in the story. There are ten of you who always did things together. This will be the first book of a series that will dwell on the lives of this group. This book will set the scene for the others and should be the story of the fallen warrior and his family. One person is a world traveling photojournalist who lost his fiancé during the last photo shoot to a terrorist bomb. Another of the group is a small rancher in Oklahoma who is having trouble with a larger rancher. Another is a lawyer who has hit a glass ceiling in a large Washington DC firm. Another is a police chief in a mid-sized city in the northeast who is tired of the politics of the town. Another is a small business owner who wants to expand his business. The next member of the group is a widower with a pre-teen son and the dad just won the lottery. The next member is a contractor who is tired of having to prove herself on every job. She also is a licensed architect. Another member of the group is a pharmacist who wants to own a pharmacy and is tired of working in the labs. The final member is a teacher who just earned her Master's in Library Sciences Make this first story a strong romantic interest story with several plot twists and at least two romantic interest. It should be at least 50,000-words with a strong moral, no explicit language or sex. Be sure to begin intertwining the lives of each within this story. Include part of the backstory of each character.

3. This should be the photojournalist story. He should be the oldest of the group and be the one who lived next door to the fallen warrior growing up. He did not meet him until junior high after moving to town to live with his grandparents after the death of his parents during a snowstorm. He was given a camera for his birthday the year he lost his parents. His story should show how he met and lost his finance as well as his life as a journalist. Intertwine the lives of the others as they discuss their lives after the funeral. Show his decision to accept the proposal of the newspaper owner to purchase the paper and return to the town. Provide him a romantic interest which will include one of the quirky townspeople. They should begin as friends, and he hires her to work for him until he can convince his former co-workers to come to the small town. This should be a 50,000-word romantic story with no explicit descriptions of sex or strong language. Use your fertile mind to develop this story with love showing without the explicit descriptions. Point to a possible love interest for the widow.

4. This is the small rancher's story. The rancher is married and expecting his first child. He also has inherited two cantankerous hands who teach him the business and help him with the trouble the larger rancher is giving him. He decides to move back home and gets a better offer because the realtor negotiates the deal for him. He brings everyone with him including his ranch hands. One of the ranch hands is a jokester and finds love with the diner owner of the town. The other is a serious-minded guy who would rather spend his off time reading more than anything else. His story should become part of the last book. Show the troubles that the rancher experienced and how he and his hands handled it. Tell this story from two points of view include action and suspense. Make this a 50,000-word romantic story with no cliffhangers, explicit descriptions of sex, or strong language. There should be at least two HEAs. Continue to do your world building and intertwining the lives of the ten initial friends. Show how the rancher met the warrior in the second grade and how their friendship developed. Touch on the widow's love story.

5. This is the lawyer's story. She met the warrior in the fifth grade. Detail their meeting and how she became a member of the group. She has been a DC lawyer for six years and has won every case she had. Has been passed over for a full partner for the last three years. She meets her old high school love interest after the funeral, and they begin a long-distance romance that culminates with her returning to the town and joining the law firm there. Continue to do your world building and intertwining the lives of the ten initial friends. This should be a romantic suspense 50,000-word story with no cliffhangers and include a strong moral no explicit description of sex and strong language. Continue to do your world building and intertwining the lives of the ten initial friends with the other characters in the town. Touch on the widow's love story. Make humor a part of this story.

6. This is the police chief's story. His life during his childhood was hard, and he got into a lot of trouble until the Sherriff of the town saved him from his abusive father. Develop the relationship between the sheriff and the young man, and show how he and the other ten became such a close group. During his senior year, the father caught him unawares one night and tried to kill him because he was living with the sheriff. What happened next? This incident is the middle of the story. Complete your worldbuilding with details concerning the others and how he is prepared to return to the town because the sheriff wants to retire. Create his love story with one of the townspeople who came to the town after he left. This person should be a relative of one of the townspeople. This story should be a romantic suspense story of at least 50,000 words with a strong moral. Include at least one more love interest in the story. Touch on the widow's love story. No cliffhangers.

7. This is the small business owner's story. He has always been the one who found positive ways for the group to earn money, so it is no surprise that he is successful. He has created a company that has expanded into four franchises and he is ready to expand to another area. He comes to town with his current girlfriend who is a prima donna and does not like any of his friends or the town. She tries to get him to leave right after the funeral, and he refuses, so she gets one of the deputies to drive her to the city and catches a plane back to California. Provide his backstory and how he became part of the group and what he has done. His business should be so successful that when the mayor joins one of the conversations she plants the idea in his head to expand his business to this town. The mayor also hints that this is her last term and when elections roll around she hopes one of the friends will consider running. She has been elected the last ten times and feels sure that if she supported whoever runs they will get elected. During your world building create the story of the business owner and the realtor. They can be slightly antagonistic toward each other because he wants to get the building across the street from her present location and she also wants that building. She should also have a preteen son who likes the business owner. He takes her son to see several business that could be expanded with the proper management. This story should be a 50,000-word romantic story without a cliffhanger no explicit descriptions of sex or strong language. Include a moral and a happily ever after.

8. This is the lottery winning father's story. Continue your world building by providing his backstory, how and when he joined the group. What happened to his wife, why he is increasingly aware that his son is suffering from her loss and needs a change of scenery. Research loss and grief in children and include information in this story. The father did the scratch and win on a dare from his son when they stopped in a gas station for gas. The son connects with several of the teens in town during the week they are there for the funeral, and the father becomes interested in the mayoral election. He and the mayor spend a lot of time together discussing things, and the mayor's secretary is the go-between. After returning home he and the secretary keep the phone calls flowing, first as the go-between then eventually they talk a lot more personally. Soon they begin meeting at places that were half the distance between the two living towns. The son would join them on some of these trips until soon they became a cohesive group yet not a family. The son also keeps in touch with the guys he met. Bring the story forward to them moving back and buying a house there and him making the leap to become the new mayor. The mayor should visit his home and meet his father. This should generate three love stories, two of them ending in HEAs. This story should be written as a 50,000-word romantic story without a cliffhanger no explicit descriptions of sex or strong language. Include a moral and lots of humor. Perhaps the photojournalist can get married in this story as well.

9. This is the story of the general contractor. She has developed her skills from working with her father who was a handyman for the town who retired and left a void. The daughter goes to college for two years but finds more enjoyment in the building process and starts her business in the college town. She occasionally comes home and has sent crews to do the work that her father can no longer do. The mayor gets her alone at the reception and plants the idea of making her headquarters in the town and sending crews to other towns. She also reconnects with one o the guys she met on one of her visits. Develop this into an HEA. He should have a back story that includes the loss of a wife and child. They were killed during a storm that ravaged the town they were living in. Develop their story slowly and intertwine several of the other's story in this one. Be sure to create the events that led her to be a part of this group. Where did she learn her skill in making people like her after finding out she is a woman? Include several incidents where she encounters people who have problems hiring her after they find out she is a woman. Give her a name that can be male or female or use initials. It should be 50,000 words long told from at least two points of view. No cliffhangers. Use your imagination to carry the story forward. Include humor and dialogue to move the story along. Include more of the widow's story. Highlight something that the children did to remember their dad. Such as designing a metal sculpture that would be displayed in the town square.

10. This should be the pharmacist's story. She will be the cousin of a lottery winner. Weave their stories in with the others. She has worked in a lab for the past ten years and was passed over for a promotion because of politics. She feels her ethnicity has something to do with it. She has outperformed everyone who interviewed for the internal promotion. But she is true to her faith and understands that God has something else for her to do. She will spend a month in town using up her vacation time that she has not taken for the past two years. She also is considering venturing into owning her own pharmacy. She does not want to remain in the same town she is in now so is open to the possibility of returning to the home town. How does her story work itself into her returning home and also fulfilling her dream of owning her own pharmacy? How and when did she become a part of the group? She grew up in the town since her parents moved there when she was an arm baby. Create a love interest for her and help her choose her destiny by staying in the town. Be sure to develop her backstory as to college attendance and other factors that led her to corporate America first rather than being just a pharmacist. This story should be a romantic comedy story, told from two points of view with no cliffhangers no strong language and no explicit descriptions of sex. It should be at least 50,000 words and two settings.

11. This should be the teacher's story. Remember she is going to fall for one of the ranch hands. Continue your worldbuilding including memories and flashbacks to how her journey began. Provide the backstory for the ranch hand and why he is still alone at age forty. He will be at least ten years older than she is. Create a disaster that involves the whole town and includes each of the ten friends in this story. There should be no explicit descriptions of sex and strong language. This should be a 50,000-word romantic story told from two points of view. Make the town itself a strong secondary character. Be sure to include humor and all of the secondary characters that you have built into the story so far. Their love story should come about by accident. Allow this to be a satisfactory ending but leave room for more stories to come. The widow's story should also be included in this one. Perhaps being the introduction to the next book in the series.

12. Your group has been in a war of espionage for several years, and each time you get close to discovering the main person behind the war you are foiled, and he escapes. This time you work a different strategy and set up a phony headquarters that each of your known operatives come and goes through the building. Your undercover operatives never show their faces. You have come to understand that there is either a mole in your group or someone is talking too much unaware that they are being observed. After several months of working in the location, it is attacked. You have planted cameras and listening devices all over the compound. Some obvious, some slightly hidden and some well-hidden with only three people knowing their location. During the attack, it appears that all operatives have left the house and are fighting. The command center is in another location, and the three of you are observing the fight, when someone walks into the building and begins looking around. He locates the cameras and ensures he is not on them. He looks through files and desk drawers. Laughs at what he believes are your attempts at security. In the meantime you are observing and recording him. He feels so confident that your team will not return until he is finished that he sits and has a cup of coffee, removes a card from his pocket and sprays it with something then places it under one of the items in the room. Picks up his phone and sends the signal to his people to stop fighting then strolls out. What happened next? This is the middle of the story. Do your world building to show who is fighting, why they are fighting and what each character is all about. Ensure that dialogue drives the story. This should be a 50,000-word romantic suspense story told from two points of view. Include humor and no cliffhangers. Try to limit explicit descriptions of sex

and strong language. Include several locations.

13. A corrupt police officer stages a shootout in which he kills his partner who discovered what he was doing. The dead officer's wife is the corrupt officer's sister. She has been entrusted with the facts and evidence of her brother's duplicity. Her husband told her to look in the last drawer of the file cabinet and open the locked box hidden there if he was ever killed. What happens next? What is the back ` story? Fill in the details about what came before this incident. Does the wife confront her brother or does she report him? Use dialogue to drive the story. Show her conflict and anger. Research police corruption and paint the picture of how her brother got started on that path. Create the story where he is discovered, but the guy who is paying him off thinks he turned him in and shoots him. This should be a 50,000-word romantic suspense story told from two points of view. Include strong secondary characters and an HEA. No explicit descriptions of sex or strong language. Mild violence is important to drive the story.

14. This is the story of a couple who took on the son of a woman who was very old and died when she gave birth. The couple has lived as a team or twenty years and are set in their ways but are willing to do what is necessary to rear the child correctly. This is the middle of the story. What happened before? Develop the story and tell it from the point of view of the mother and the couple Give their backstory and show the relationship between the three. Be sure the story includes the love story o the biological parents. Continue the story until the child grows up and tries to find his biological father and what happened to his mother. The private investigator that he hires should be his love interest. Develop their story and intertwine their lives during the discovery of his biological parents. This should be a 50,000-word or more romantic story. Include a moral and humor. Dialogue should drive the story and try to limit explicit descriptions of sex or strong language.

15. Sarah, we are over $200,000 in debt, and I have no way to get us out. I lost my job two weeks ago and the money I gave you last week was my last paycheck. I have been praying and trying to figure out how to tell you. God told me last night that I must tell you. Please say something. What does she say? Develop the story to show what happened before this incident. Continue the story to show what happened after this incident. Make this a romantic suspense story and have the man involved with shady characters that targeted him and he was in too deep before he discovered what type of characters he was involved with in this enterprise. Include humor and a moral and no cliffhangers if you want to make this part of a series.

16. You are a member of DEA and have worked for years to stem the tide of illegal drugs when suddenly All drugs, legal and illegal, suddenly cease to have any effect on their users. Write about what ensues. You and a scientist are assigned to discover what is happening. Tell it from two points of view. Be sure to include secondary characters that help drive the story. Dialogue should move the story along not descriptions. Make this a romantic suspense story with two HEAs. Make this at least 40,000-words include humor throughout the story. There should be no explicit descriptions of sex and strong language.

17. A secret society has been causing problems in your town. You have been gone for four years and return to a different town than you left. When you visit a diner, you are mistaken for a member of a cult, when you accidentally imitate their secret greeting. You are taken to the headquarters and interrogated. There are three people who seem to be leading the cult. One of them gives you a look that says trust me. This should be a 50,000-word romantic suspense story. Tell the story from two points of view. There should be no cliffhangers and no explicit descriptions of sex and strong language. Include the HEA for your main character and one of the members of the cult. During your world building include how the cult got started and some of the havoc they caused. Your hero should eventually dismantle the cult. The leader should be one of the town members who got greedy then got in over his head.

18. You are the captain of a spaceship that has been sent to help the people of earth continue their existence since their sun is dying. You can only carry 100,000 people to safety. How will humanity decide who gets to be a passenger? Your secondary character is the President o the United States which now includes Canada and South America. This is the middle of the story. What came before? How does it end? Do your world building surrounding how man caused such destruction because they were trying to tap the sun's energy. Make this a complete novel of at least 50,000 words. No strong language or explicit descriptions of sex. As you write the story, include scenes that should point to how greed came into play. Include at least two morals and two HEAs.

19. During a blackout, all of the music of the world disappears. When the blackout ends what happens? Your main character is a great composer who no longer knows what music is. Your secondary characters are three individuals who have music in their heads but can't get it out. An alliance is formed. What happens next?. Build your world first around how people took music for granted and stopped attending concerts or buying the music then end it with these four saving the world of music and also two HEAs. Make this a complete novel of at least 50,000 words. No strong language or explicit descriptions of sex. As you write the story, include scenes that point to a sinister plot that erased music from the world. Be sure to make dialogue the factor that drives the story. Tell it from an omniscient point of view.

20. You are an online gamer creator. You have created a game so realistic that suddenly the computer starts talking back to you and tells you how to arrange the game. Before long a man who says he is from the government shows up at your door. Your game has been interacting in real life situations. This is the middle of the story. Why are you so frightened that you only interact with people through the computer? What caused this? Make this person super smart but traumatized. In his late twenties. Build your world so that we understand what is going on in his world and how he is stuck and can't get out. Create a romance that will not only help him come out of the house but help save the world from total disaster. Make this a complete novel of at least 50,000 words. No strong language or explicit descriptions of sex. No cliffhangers.

20. Four people are swept up into an alien ship and transported to another world. When they arrive, they discover that they are headed to a prison camp. The begin to entertain the captain and crew with stories each has heard since childhood. This causes the captain to reevaluate his decision. Perhaps they can be useful in another way.Tell this from four points of view. Blend the stories to make one story. Include, humor, mystery, action and several HEAs. This should be a full length at least 50,000-word novel. Build your world around why the ship came to earth in the first place, then the space travel and finally the alien world. Create exciting secondary characters and develop the love relationships so that the four become a part of the alien world and helps the people in charge find a better way to build things rather than capturing prisoners and forcing them into labor camps. No explicit descriptions of sex, cliffhanger, or strong language.

22. You heard there would be a huge earthquake to-morrow, but nobody will listen. Today is April Fool's Day. What happened next? Where did you get your information? What is your occupation? Why do you think people should believe you in spite of the day's designation? This should be a paranormal story. Create at least two HEA. Create a world that is filled with unique devices. You are what type of paranormal? Are you hidden or does the world know about paranormal beings? Make this an action-adventure story. This should be a full novel with at least 50,000 words. There should be no explicit descriptions of sex or strong language. Let your creative mind tell the story without this but let them be alluded to if you must. No cliffhangers.

23. You and a co-worker are standing in line at the local diner when suddenly a loud commotion occurs in the kitchen, and the cook runs out shouting and runs out the door. Nothing else happens for about five minutes while you and the rest wait to determine what happened. No one comes from the back. This is the beginning of the story. Build a world that surrounds the two who are waiting. What disturbed the cook? What happens next? Include humor, suspense, and an HEA. No strong language or explicit descriptions of sex. Make this at least 50,000-words with a strong moral.

24. You broke up with your fiancé three years ago. Moved to New York, started a new career and tried to put him out of your mind and heart. You go for an extended visit to an aunt who runs a bed and breakfast and three days into your visit your x- fiancé shows up. He is running from someone and they believe you have what he was supposed to have. Tell this from one point of view but as an observer and not a character in the story. Make this a 50,000-word romantic suspense novel with at least two HEAs, humor, suspense, action, and at least two moral decisions. There should be no strong description of sex or strong language.

25. You are a photographer who is on assignment at a remote cabin. You are assigned to photograph the animals and vegetation of the area. One day you are taking pictures and capture a scene that blows your mind. What happens after this is totally under your control, tell it from two points of view. This should be an action adventure, romantic suspense and filled with humor, a little drama, and lots of expressions of friendship. There should be an HEA and no explicit descriptions of sex or strong language. Make this a 50,000-word novel that could easily be part of a series.

26. You have been sitting at a table in a restaurant for the past half hour waiting for a client who is running late. When your client arrives, he is angry because his secretary forgot to tell him about the meeting. She has been doing a lot of that lately. You know why the secretary is doing these things but can't tell him. This is the middle of the story. What happened before this? Make this a 50,000-word story with at least two HEAs and several morals. Include humor and avoid explicit descriptions of sex and strong language.

27. While walking down the street, you encounter two men who refuse to get out of your way. Both are known to you. Suddenly the larger guy reaches out and grabs your arm. He whispers something in your ear that turns your green then walks away. You slip on the wall. Another man comes up and asks after your health? He explains that he saw what happened and wanted to know if he should call the cops. This is the middle of the story. What came before? Build a world around these two characters that will show both of their circumstances. This should be a story filled with humor, love, sacrifice, betrayal, and a happily ever after for both of them. Include several morals and no explicit descriptions of sex or strong language.

28. Your marriage of five years changes suddenly. One day you are riding on a small plane and by the time you get off you are blind. You and your partner are both world renown painters. How does the relationship change? This is the middle o the story. What happened before this? Research blind painters and how they got over the disability. Research stress on the marriage as well. Weave your findings into the story. Do they have children? Make the story exciting and show how the couple overcame the disability and grew stronger. Make this a 50,000-word story with at least two HEAs and several morals. Include humor and avoid explicit descriptions of sex and strong language.

29. A dream come true: Your main character dreams about picking up the same anonymous hitchhiker three nights in a row. The next day, she sees the same hitchhiker on her commute home from work. She pulls over. This is the middle of the story. What happened before these events? Build a world around these two characters that involve dreams coming true. Perhaps make the woman a dream researcher before she suddenly becomes the object of her own research. Include humor, drama, several plot twists, and of course the HEA. Avoid excessive descriptions of sex and strong language. Tell this from two points of view.

30. Your mother dies then three days after the funeral your father dies. You have just turned 20 and have lived at home all of your life. Your job is work from home, so you answer the phone every time it rings. You establish friendships with the telemarketers who call. They are never able to give their pitch because you start asking them questions. Eventually, they stop calling you except for one. He likes your voice. What happens next? Be sure to tell the backstory throughout your story. Let the reader in on how your life was before your parents' deaths while weaving in a love story between you and the telemarketer. Include humor, drama, several plot twists, and of course the HEA. Avoid excessive descriptions of sex and strong language. This one will be from the female point of view.

About The Author

Marier Farley is a retired educator and lives by the motto "Jesus Christ is the head of my life." She began writing stories in the first grade and has not stopped writing since.

Having retired from 37 years of teaching in the public-school systems of the South, Ms. Farley has learned the power of prayer by experience.

She has discovered after traveling extensively on the North American continent that time spent with the giver outweighs even the gift.

The author has gone down the road of accumulating wealth in knowledge, spirituality and being comfortable. She watches TV, works on her computer, and enjoys popular music, in other words, she is a real person. Prayer is for real people like her and you.

Come and see.

Marier Farley

Other Books By Marier Farley

Undercover A Keith Daniels Mystery
How Do You Respond To The Promises Of God?
A Father For Me, Meghan (To Love Wisely Book 4)
To Love Wisely Or Not At All: Book Two in the To Love Wisely Series
Prayers of Gratitude: Book 2 of Prayer Works Series
Prayer Changes Things (Prayer Works Book 1)
It's Time To Move: Making a Change Towards Giving God Glory
Harnessing The Power of Prayer
30 Prompts 30 Stories Books 1, 2, 3, and 4
Coming December 2018, It Came to Pass. A book filled with stories of how God brought people through circumstances they could not overcome on their own. It is also a devotional with scriptures and prayers.
Other titles may be found on Amazon under the author Marier Farley or Karen Stevens

One Last Thing...

If you enjoyed this book or found it useful, I'd be very grateful if you'd post a short review on Amazon. Your support does make a difference, and I read all the reviews personally so I can get your feedback and make thi0s book even better.

Made in the USA
Middletown, DE
24 November 2018